My Emotions
Emosyon Mwen Yo

SCARED
PÈ

A Crabtree Roots Book
Yon Liv Crabtree Rasin

AMY CULLIFORD
JEAN-PIERRE GASTON

Crabtree Publishing
crabtreebooks.com

School-to-Home Support for Caregivers and Teachers

This book helps children grow by letting them practice reading. Here are a few guiding questions to help the reader with building his or her comprehension skills. Possible answers appear here in red.

Before Reading:

- What do I think this book is about?
    - *This book is about feeling scared.*
    - *This book is about what feeling scared looks or feels like.*

- What do I want to learn about this topic?
    - *I want to learn what to do if I feel scared.*
    - *I want to learn what feeling scared looks like.*

During Reading:

- I wonder why...
    - *I wonder why we cry when we are scared.*
    - *I wonder why trying new things is scary.*

- What have I learned so far?
    - *I have learned that scared is an emotion.*
    - *I have learned that some people yell when they are scared.*

After Reading:

- What details did I learn about this topic?
    - *I have learned that it is good to tell someone you are scared.*
    - *I have learned that everyone can feel scared about something.*

- Read the book again and look for the vocabulary words.
    - *I see the word **hide** on page 6 and the word **storms** on page 8. The other vocabulary words are found on page 14.*

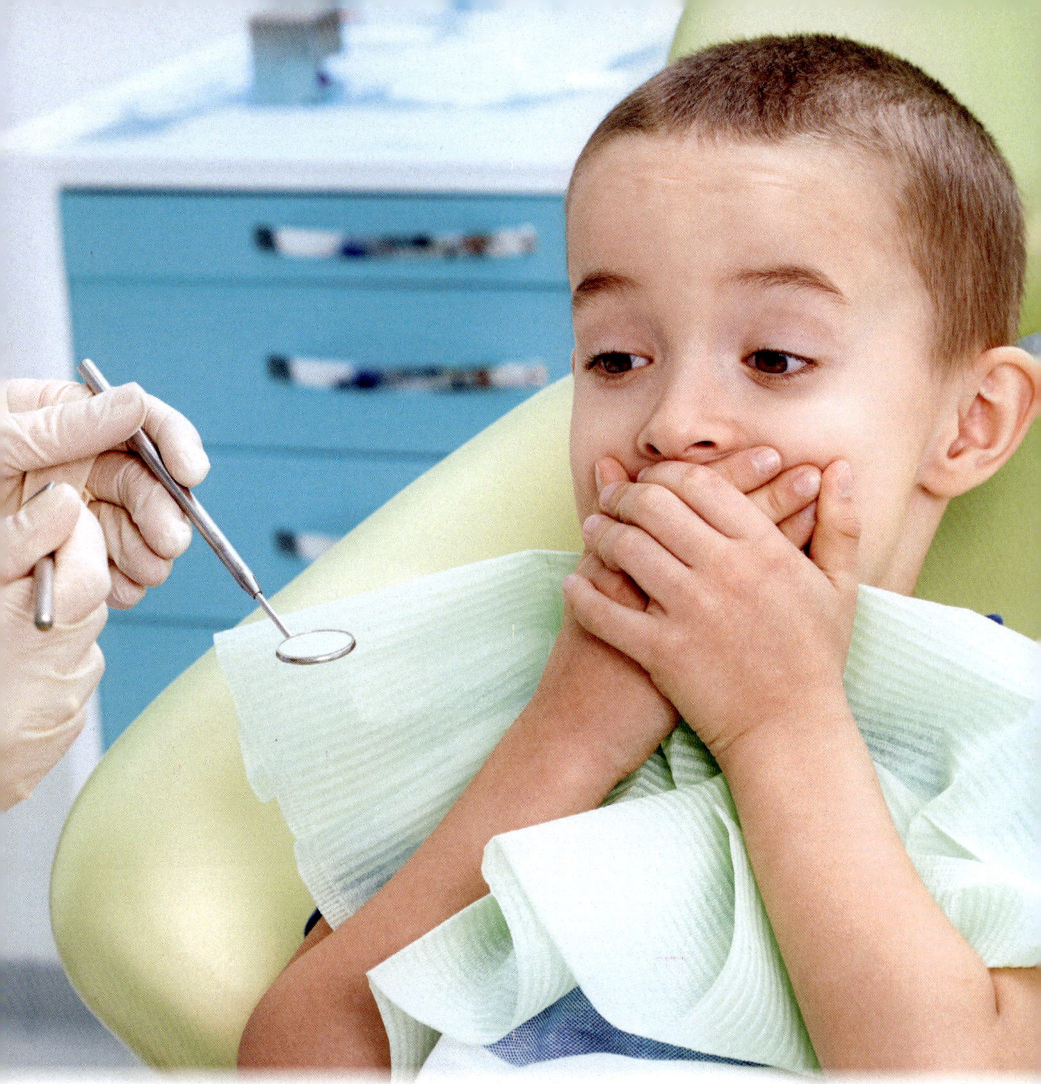

What **scares** you?

Ki sa ki fè ou **pè**?

I am scared of the **dark**.

Mwen pè nan fè **nwa**.

I **hide** when I am scared.

Mwen ale **kache** lè mwen pè.

I am scared of **storms**.

Mwen pè **tanpèt**.

I **cry** when am I am scared.

Mwen **kriye** lè mwen pè.

I go find my **mom** when I am scared.

Mwen ale jwenn **manman** mwen lè mwen pè.

What scares you?

Ki sa ki fè ou pè?

Words to Know
Mo pouw Konnen

cry
kriye

dark
nwa

hide
kache

mom
manman

scares
pè

storms
tonpèt

38 Words

What **scares** you?

I am scared of the **dark**.

I **hide** when I am scared.

I am scared of **storms**.

I **cry** when I am scared.

I go find my **mom** when I am scared.

What scares you?

38 mo

Kisa ki fè ou **pè**?

Mwen pè nan fè **nwa**.

Mwen ale **kache** lè mwen pè.

Mwen pè **tanpèt**.

Mwen **kriye** lè mwen pè.

Mwen ale jwenn **manman** mwen lè mwen pè.

Ki sa ki fè ou pè?

My Emotions

SCARED

Emosyon Mwen Yo

PÈ

Crabtree Publishing

crabtreebooks.com 800-387-7650

Paperback 9781039624603
Ebook (pdf) 9781039625440
Epub 9781039625020

Printed in the U.S.A./CP102025

Library and Archives Canada Cataloguing in Publication
Available at the Library and Archives Canada

Library of Congress Cataloging-in-Publication Data
Available at the Library of Congress

Published in Canada
Crabtree Publishing
616 Welland Avenue
St. Catharines, Ontario
L2M 5V6

Published in the United States
Crabtree Publishing
347 Fifth Avenue
Suite 1402-145
New York, NY 10016

Written by: Amy Culliford
Designed by: Rhea Wallace
Series Development: James Earley
Proofreader: Ellen Rodger
Educational Consultant: Marie Lemke M.Ed.
Translator: Jean-Pierre Gaston
Production manager: Candice Campbell

Photographs: Shutterstock: Juan Pablo Gonzaález: cover; TY IIm: p. 1; Aleksandr Rybalko: p. 3, 14; Kryzhov: p. 5, 14; justoomm: p. 7, 14; HelloRF Zcool: p. 8, 14; fizkes: p. 9, 14; Inna Ska: p. 13